I love reading

Giant Dinosaurs

by Monica Hughes

Consultant: Dougal Dixon

CONTENTS

Words in **bold** are explained in the glossary.

Dinosaur giants

Long ago **dinosaurs** and other giant creatures lived on land.

There were giant creatures in the sea . . .

. . . and in the air, too.

Heaviest meat-eating dinosaur

T. rex may have been the heaviest **meat-eater**.

Size

6

It weighed as much as
two large elephants.

It ate large and small animals.

Tyrannosaurus rex
tie-ran-o-sor-us rex

Biggest meat-eating dinosaur

Giganotosaurus was one of the biggest meat-eaters.

Size

It was longer than T. rex,
but not as heavy.

Giganotosaurus
jie-gan-ot-o-sor-us

Heaviest plant-eating dinosaur

The heaviest
dinosaur of all
weighed as much
as 14 elephants!

Size

It had a small head and
a small brain.

Argentinosaurus
ar-jun-teen-o-sor-us

11

Tallest plant-eating dinosaur

The tallest dinosaur was 22 metres tall. Its neck was 16 metres long.

Sauroposeidon
saw-ro-po-si-don

Tail

It had a small head, thick legs and a short tail.

Neck

Size

Biggest flying creature

The biggest **flying creature** was the size of a small aeroplane.

It had a long neck and long **jaws**.

Size

It had a crest on its head.

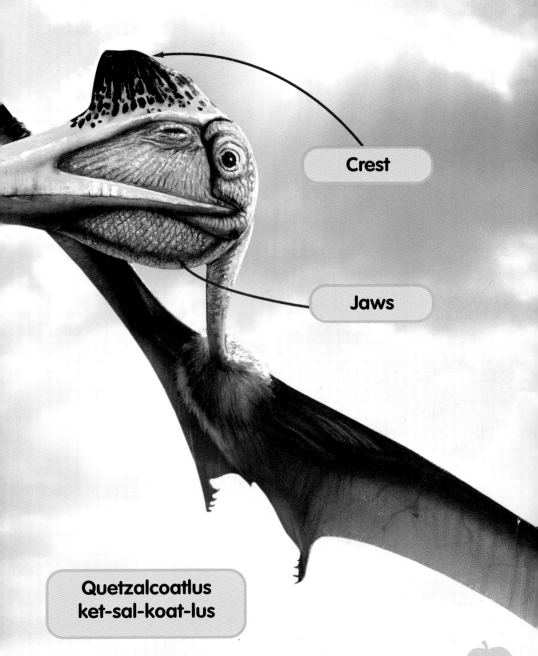

Crest

Jaws

Quetzalcoatlus
ket-sal-koat-lus

Biggest
sea creature

The biggest **sea creature** was 24 metres long. It had long jaws and sharp teeth.

Liopleurodon
lee-o-plur-o-don

It was fierce!

Size

Sea creature with the longest neck

Look at this creature's neck.
It is much longer than
a giraffe's neck.

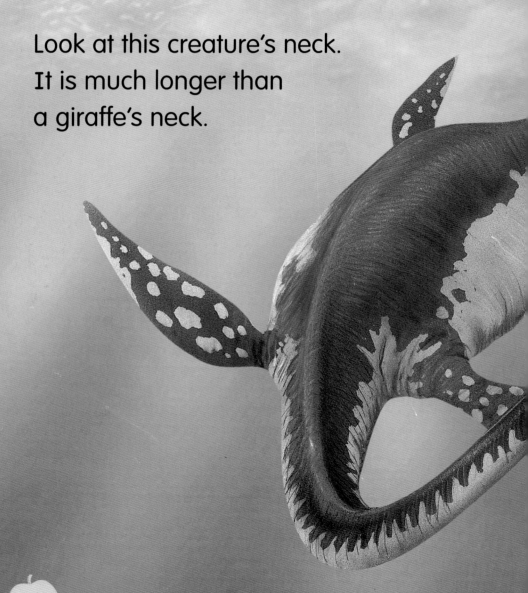

This sea creature was 14 metres long.

Elasmosaurus
ee-las-mo-sor-us

Size

Biggest crocodile?

Deinosuchus lived at the time of the dinosaurs. It might be the biggest crocodile that has ever lived.

Size

Deinosuchus

Crocodile

It was so big it could eat a dinosaur!

Deinosuchus
dyn-o-soo-cus

Glossary

dinosaurs
Lizard-like animals that lived a long time ago.

flying creature
An animal that flew in the sky during the time of the dinosaurs.

jaws
The part of the
mouth that holds
the teeth.

meat-eater
An animal that
eats other
animals.

sea creature
An animal that
swam in the sea
during the time of
the dinosaurs.

Index

An Hachette UK Company
www.hachette.co.uk
Copyright © Octopus Publishing Group Ltd 2013
First published in Great Britain in 2008 by TickTock, an imprint of Octopus Publishing Group Ltd,
Endeavour House, 189 Shaftesbury Avenue, London WC2H 8JY.
www.octopusbooks.co.uk

ISBN 978 1 84696 755 9

Printed in China
1 3 5 7 9 10 8 6 4 2

Picture credits (t=top, b=bottom, c=centre, l-left, r=right, OFC= outside front cover)
Lisa Alderson: 1, 6-7, 12-13; John Alston: 6l, 8, 20l; Natural History Museum: 17c; Bob Nicholls: 16-17, 23c; Luis Rey: 2, 4, 5b,
14-15, 18-19, 20-21, 23t, 22b, 23b; Science Photo Library: 9; Shutterstock: 5t, 14bl, 14br, 19b, 20b; Simon Mendez: 10-11, 22t.